WILSON AND WHITWORTH,

PRINTING IN ALL ITS BRANCHES Neatly and Promptly Executed

"EXPRESS" OFFICE, 201 AND 203, HIGH STREET NORTH, EAST HAM

THE BOROUGH OF EAST HAM, WEST HAM AND

Stratford Express.

PUBLISHED MONDAY, WEDNESDAY AND FRIDAY.

Telephones:
East Ham Office—EAST HAM 529.
Stratford Office—EAST 932.

Telephones:
East Ham Office—EAST HAM 529.
Stratford Office—EAST 932.

Bygone
EAST HAM

The Town Hall, 1920s.

Bygone EAST HAM

Brian Evans

Phillimore

1993

Published by
PHILLIMORE & CO. LTD.
Shopwyke Manor Barn, Chichester, Sussex

ISBN0 85033 877 8

Printed and bound in Great Britain by
BIDDLES LTD.
Guildford, Surrey

To Susan and my friends in local history

List of Illustrations

Frontispiece: The Town Hall, 1920s

Acknowledgements

The author would like to thank the following for all the help they have given with either the text or the illustrations: James Hawes, the Governors and Trustees of the Passmore Edwards Museum, the London Borough of Newham Local History librarian, the London Borough of Redbridge Local History librarian, and the Port of London Authority.

As Far as the Eye Can See: Memories of the 1860s recorded by J. Charters

In the 1860s East Ham was an area of intensive cultivation, with crops of root vegetables stretching across the horizon as far as the eye could see. Beyond the ancient parish church to the south, were marshes which were used for grazing cattle. The marshes stretched from Barking in the east, Plaistow in the west and with the river Thames to the south. The old church and its burial ground stood on the dividing line between marsh and arable land which marked the boundary from time immemorial.

The road southward had always been known as the Manor Way, a narrow winding lane with sluice ditches on both sides, leading right down to the river, a causeway sloping into the water. Only one house stood between the church and the river and that was a humble farm, not quite halfway along the road to North Woolwich. A traveller to Woolwich on a dark and foggy night found his journey on the only possible route a hazardous one, for if he forgot to provide himself with an adequate lantern he would probably stumble into one of the ditches and, likely as not, struggle out the wrong side, finding to his chagrin that in order to restart his journey he must give himself another wetting.

In season North Woolwich gardens were a favourite pleasure resort for East Londoners, who arrived in great numbers to sample the variety of amusements to be found beneath its arbours. One attraction was the largest dancing platform in London. To have paid a visit to these gardens in spring when the buds of the chestnut trees were transformed into young jewel-like leaves was a unique experience. The constantly changing scenes of shipping on the river heightened the joy of such a trip.

Northwards from St Mary's church Manor Way led to Wanstead Flats, through fields which were used to grow market-garden crops. Between the church and the Barking Road (then New Road) several clusters of houses were to be seen, the most notable being the six almshouses which stood well back from the road, in their own grounds. They had been founded by Giles Breame, for three poor people of the parish and three poor people of Bottisham, Cambridgeshire. The *White Horse* inn was the only dwelling house in East Ham with a thatched roof. A few farmhouses and the ruins of a very large house (the Clock House), of which the wrought-iron entrance gates were all that remained, were nearby. The Clock House had been the residence of the Burges family. Apparently when the house was abandoned it was instructed that the gates should be left standing until they collapsed. Presumably there was some symbolic intention in this akin to the ideas of the Old Testament, this being the only book that most villagers would have knowledge of.

If one continued northwards the Barking Road (New Road) was reached. A tollhouse stood near what later became the Provincial Bank. No vehicle could pass east or west along the crossroads without paying a toll. Gates and posts running as far as the hedges at the side of the road barred the passage of any vehicles. What fine gymnastic exercise these barriers made for the youth of the day! Halfway between the New Road and Wakefield Street on the east side of the road was a old-established builder's yard and workshops belonging to Stokes. Opposite, was a well-known blacksmith's shop, called Moss's, where many of the area's horses were shod. In the meadow adjoining the forge a crowd of guinea fowls were usually to be seen and especially heard, for their cackling was quite the noisiest sound in the street. Nearer Wakefield Street and next door to the village post office stood the wheelwright's shop where farm wagons and carts were built and repaired. Opposite Wakefield Street stood Colliers, one of the two bakeries in the parish. Next door to the baker lived Perry, the only butcher.

Further north stood a cluster of houses known as the Harrow, taking its name, no doubt, from an old-fashioned licensed house standing on the east side of the road. Nearly opposite the *Harrow* was Pizzey's, the harnessmakers.

At the foot of the railway station bridge, on the south side, there were a number of trees, looking just like Christmas trees. East Ham railway station was a very small building on the down platform; no cover at all was available on the up platform. Passengers for this side were warned by a porter who called out 'Cross over please for the up train'. A flight of wooden stairs had to be negotiated to get down onto the gravelled platform from the road. Once on the platform, as Stokes, the East Ham historian remarks, the traveller was likely to be impressed by the gardening prowess of the station master, evidenced by the profusion of flowers on the banks. John Barnes, the station master, was a popular person in the community and proud of his family of eight or nine. At this time many local families had six or more children. The road known as Jews Farm Lane began north of the station, running eastwards from Northend Corner. The lane terminated at sheds which were used by the firm of Crosse and Blackwell for peeling onions, before they were pickled. In the season hundreds of women and girls were employed there, the strong smell of onions reaching great distances.

From Northend Corner the road north was known as White Post Lane, which continued as far as Wanstead Flats, deep ditches running on either side. The most famous of the three large houses which stood near Northend Corner was Woodhouse, the home of the Gingell family. Although the Gingells were Quakers they took a great interest in the parish, the clock in St John's church being donated by them. They also maintained two Sunday schools, one at Wall End and another for older boys which was held in a farmhouse opposite the post office. Sunday school treats were sometimes held in meadows adjoining Woodhouse.

The Romford Road was reached at White Post; this was always a wide road. An extension of the road northwards led to Wanstead Flats. On the edge of the Flats was Manor House, once the residence of the Fry family but since converted into an industrial school. Gypsy Lane, with its famously deep ditches, turned off the Romford Road and ran westwards leading to, and terminating at, St George-in-the-East industrial school.

Green Street began at the industrial school and ran southwards to Morley's Corner, Barking Road. In addition to the Castle (then known as Morley's Castle) there were only two other cottages in Green Street. The Castle had housed a number of notable families, the Nevilles, who were related to the royal house, being the most famous. Running eastwards from Morley's Corner (known later as Boleyn Corner) the Barking Road to the tollgate was a wide road with ditches running alongside it, and only a farmhouse near the Corner. Further east, by the tollgate, standing well-back from the main road, stood a very fine mansion known as East Ham House. Where the town hall now stands the lonely Barking Road ran through open country to the Roding boundary. Halfway along this road, in the hamlet of Wall End, stood some two score houses. From here to the river the land was very flat and low and flooding was common.

In the 1860s Wakefield Street, in the main village contained about 40 cottages and three larger houses, the finest being Temple House. The old workhouse was situated in Wakefield Street, although by this time it was being used as the village school. Red Post Lane ran from the *Green Man* inn to the Romford Road and high hedges on either side were a landmark. Three large houses stood near the *Green Man.* Plashet House stood within extensive grounds and a large park, and had several lodge gates, one near St George's school in Green Street. The house was well-known as being the one-time residence of the philanthropist Elizabeth Fry. A pond known as Ramsden's was the delight of small boys on Saturdays. White Horse Lane ran from the house of that name to Morley's Corner, Barking Road. In the lane was a famous spring named 'Miller's Well', water from which was said to cure many ailments, particularly eye afflictions. In Plashet Grove, near to the *Green Man* inn, stood the Round House, which comprised four dwellings, the entrance doors of each facing the four points of the compass.

The parish church was a small 12th-century building which had survived largely intact. Passing under the rare Norman arch, the building was entered by the west door under the tower. A fine marble font more than two centuries old could be seen, the name of the donor and date were easily read, and with it a cover given in memory of a late vicar. The font was placed just inside the door on the north side. The church also contained a few good stained glass windows. In the chancel the remains of some tooth arches could be seen, with a beautiful apse at the east end. Behind the altar were the kneeling figures of some members of the Neville family. There were many tablets, most of them readable, some indistinct frescoes on the walls, two very fine brasses on the floor, several monuments to the Heigham Bondishes and the Burges family. At this period the church was furnished with high-backed pews. A large one, presumably once the squire's, near the chancel contained a fireplace. (The clergy vestry at the south porch has since been restored.) A large gallery was placed over the west entrance. An old-fashioned barrel organ led the singing during services. In the belfry, although there were frames for six bells, only two remained. Out in the churchyard several quaint 18th-century gravestones provided information about an older generation, and a certain amount of fine wrought ironwork decorated the vaults. This church was the only place of worship in the parish for morning service. Until St John's church was built in 1864 evening services had been held in the large hall belonging to the day school in Wakefield Street. The old church's gallery would be filled with Sunday School children, who would march from the schoolroom in Vicarage Lane. At service times a number of carriages would appear in the quiet lane, bringing the farmers and gentry of the village. Then the little church would be filled with worshippers, the services being both a spiritual and social occasion.

*****

What might later generations think about the amenities provided by the village? Such rurality had its price. There were no public lights in the parish, no pavements, no water mains, water had to be fetched from pumps or wells. The nearest doctor and chemist lived at Barking. People thought nothing of walking the lanes to Barking or Stratford in order to shop. Six farmers worked most of the cultivated land and employed most of the villagers, male and female – that was East Ham in the 1860s.

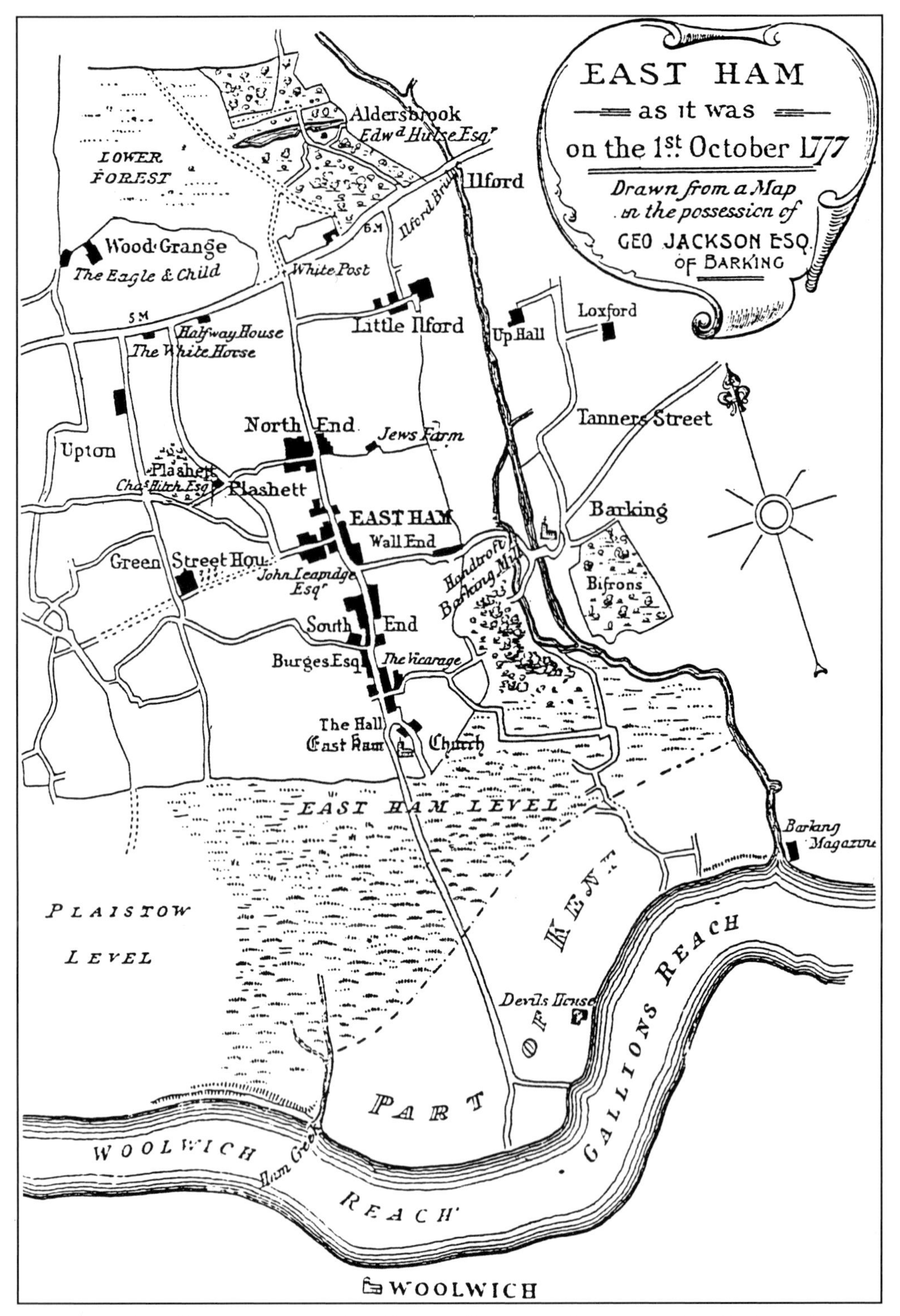

1. Redrawn from Chapman and André's 1777 map of Essex, this shows some of the distinctive features and hamlets that made up the geography of the area.

2. Plan and views of St Mary Magdalene. A postcard issued by E. P. Alderslade of East Ham.

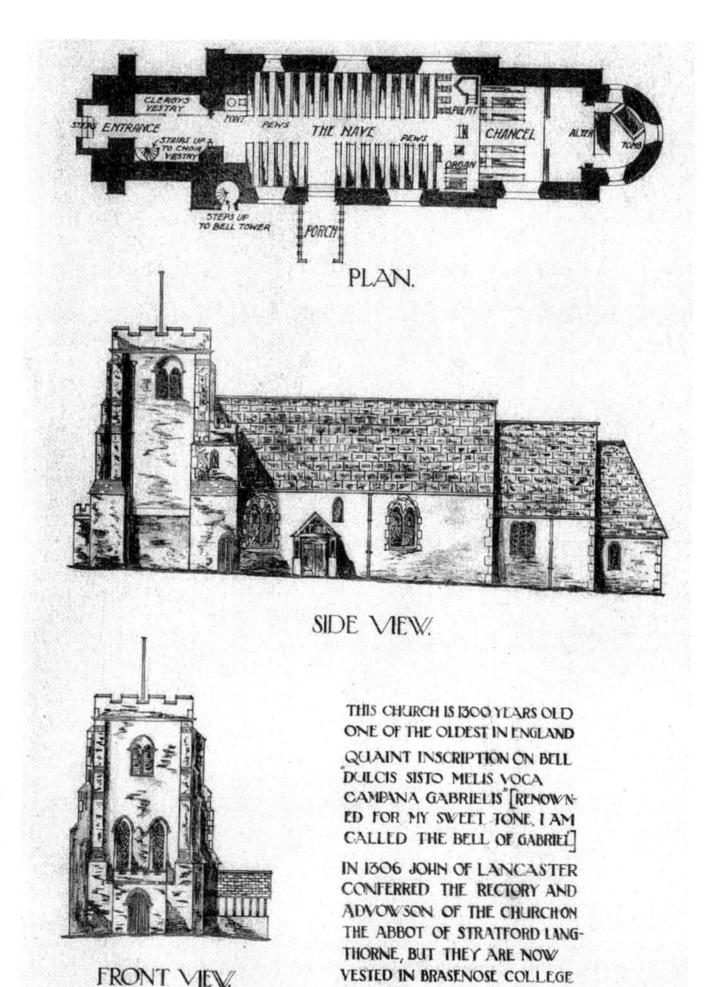

3. The church of St Mary Magdalene has one of the largest churchyards in Europe. Now bounded to the south by the busy Newham Way, it was once open to the wastes of the gull-haunted East Ham Level and the banks of the Thames. It is likely that the churchyard provided a temporary hiding place for some of the contraband which smugglers secretly brought up Manor Way. It was not unknown for the smugglers to loosen sections of the more elaborate tombs in order to conceal goods.

4. A sketch of the entrance to East Ham church showing the Roman sarcophagus and leaden coffins which were discovered in a field in December 1863, thus suggesting that there had been a Roman presence in the area.

5. In 1931, whilst repairs were being carried out to the parish church a decision was made to open up the remains of the anker-hold on the north side o the chancel. Anchorites were religious hermits who lived and died in such cells. The cell itself took the form of a lean-to shed which extended 8 or 9 ft. to the north, within which area the remains of two burials were discovered. The cell was thought to date from 1230, before which it had been a door.

6. A general view of the interior of the church. The picture dates from the early 20th-century and shows how much furniture was fitted into the compact interior at the apse end.

7. *(right)* Some of the brasses in St Mary Magdalene, which provide a key to the history of some East Ham families: a. Brass to Hester Neve, 1610, with an inscription and shield of arms. She stands upon a pedestal in an attitude of prayer, half turned to the right. She wears a broad-brimmed hat, with the crown wreathed, hood, neck ruffles, a bodice with peaked stomacher and striped sleeves, gown very widely set-off crinoline fashion from the hips and low shoes tied with bows. Both the bodice and the gown are widely open at the front, displaying the profusely embroidered under-petticoat, in the fashion of the day.

7b. *(below left)* The arms of Mary Johnson, wife of William Johnson, attractively engraved on a brass, found on her grave in the apse and dated about 1630.

7c. *(below right)* Elizabeth Heigham, brass, 1622.

8. This early 20th-century drawing depicts the north side of the chancel, showing a 12th-century wall arcade of Norman arches.

9. A drawing, dating from 1903, of the south-east view of the apse. This part of the church is apparently of later date than the oldest part of the fabric, which has suffered few alterations.

10. The font of 1639.

11. Giles Bream's almshouses mentioned in the introduction. The first of a group of the village's old buildings to be pictured.

12a. East Ham's early workhouse, built in 1804, was at Wall End towards the eastern boundary of the parish. In 1827 it was replaced by a newer, larger building in Wakefield Street. The building survived as a private dwelling into the mid-19th century.

12b. An undated picture of the second workhouse.

13. An idyllic view of Plashet House, the home of Joseph and Elizabeth Fry from 1809-29.

14. Here we see the garden front of Plashet House in 1919. Mr. and Mrs. Russel and Mrs. Talbot were well-known residents of the village.

15. The Limes in White Post Lane was one of the fine old houses of East Ham. It stood between Gladstone Avenue and East Avenue in what is now High Street North. For some years it was the home of Mr. J. T. East, the first chairman of the urban district council. It was afterwards used as a temporary library for the north part of the borough. The photograph is undated, but note the early milk float.

16. Old cottages in High Street South, survivors from the old village. This photograph was taken early this century, after the installation of a tramway standard.

17. East Ham post office in 1872.

18. The Clock House, which used to stand opposite Market Street belonged to, and was the occasional residence of, the Burges family – one of the area's oldest families. Its later dereliction is described in the introduction.

19. The Round House or Octagonal Cottage was occupied by several families. Note the pump in the foreground.

20. East Ham House stood just behind St Bartholomew's church, Barking Road and originally had its own park, approached by a fine avenue of trees, only a short distance from the turnpike. In about 1872 the house was the residence of Mr. Deputy Atkins, a member of the City Corporation. At the Lord Mayor's Show this white-haired gentleman would ride in one of the carriages. Inside the house were beautiful tapestries, rare china, clocks and paintings.

21. In the north-east of East Ham was Little Ilford, originally an independent parish with its early church.

22. Little Ilford Manor House with its distinctive cupola. This building, which was surrounded by peaceful fields, was a successor to earlier houses on the site.

23. *The Three Rabbits* public house on the Romford Road. A great market for cattle from Wales, Scotland and the north used to be held around the Wanstead Flats and the open forest just to the north, and transactions were often sealed at the *Rabbits*. It has since been rebuilt.

Civic Pride

It is said that in the reign of Edward III, East Ham contained 18 houses and 43 inhabitants. In the 1860s and '70s Elizabeth Fry's sister, Katherine, commented that East Ham 'was until recently a long and struggling village, extending from the Wanstead Flats to the Thames at North Woolwich, and apparently of little interest except to market gardeners'. The village became a town, growing to its latter size and density of population in the comparatively short period of 50 years. Most of the population increase occurred in the 20 years between 1891 and 1911. The rapid development of the borough is seen in the following statistics:

Date	Houses	Population
1861	497	2,858
1881	1,930	10,706
1891	5,818	32,718
1901	17,937	96,018
1911	25,694	133,487
1921	27,478	143,304
1931	29,602	142,394

From the latter half of the 19th century the growth of East Ham was matched by changes in local government. Before 1878 the Poor Law Guardians of West Ham Union acted as the Sanitary Authority. The rapid development of the area since that date required a frequent expansion of functions. Local governmemt in East Ham passed through a number of stages:

1878 East Ham Local Board created (Local Government Board Order)
1894 Urban District Council formed (Local Government Act)
1904 Borough status (Royal Charter incorporated)
1914 County Borough (East Ham Corporation Act)

The last promotion into the ranks of the most powerful local government bodies enabled East Ham to reach its summit as an independent unit.

24. A view of the City of London cemetery, Little Ilford, July 1856. The cemetery was created on land which had formed part of the manor of Aldersbrook. The manor passed through the hands of Henry VIII several times. By the end of the 16th century it belonged to Robert, Earl of Leicester. In the 18th century the land came into the possession of the family of Charles Lethieullier, a man very interested in local antiquities. This cemetery could be said to have been one of East Ham's first amenities!

25. A stalwart band of men – the East Ham fire brigade, 1919-21. Note the birdcage in the open window. Was the bird an advance warning system for gas?

26. An East Ham fire appliance on display at Merryweather's the manufacturers of fire protection vehicles.

EAST HAM CORPORATION

ELECTRICITY SUPPLY

ELECTRICITY for ALL PURPOSES

Up-to-Date Brilliant Lighting

Power and Heating

DON'T BE AFRAID TO COMMUNICATE WITH US
WE ARE ALWAYS AT YOUR SERVICE.

Meters and Connections Free.

Appointments may be made at any time with the Corporation Representatives, when fullest information will be given upon receipt of a card addressed to:

The . .

ENGINEER AND MANAGER,
ELECTRICITY WORKS.
NELSON STREET, EAST HAM, E.

27. A 1916 advertisement for municipal electricity would get top marks today for its attention to customer care.

28. East Ham Education Office, formerly known as the School Board Office, was housed in this handsome building, showing the importance placed on the organisation of schools and teaching. The picture dates from 1905.

29. The High Street schools in High Street South, shown here in 1905, were built in 1874 at a cost of £5,000 (this included a residence for the master). As the population of the village grew so did the size and catchment area of the schools.

30a & b. Shaftesbury Road schools before and after a fire on 25 November 1903 which damaged a large part of the roof. Luckily there were no casualties. Note the double gates, in the first picture, segregating entry and exit.

31. Hartley Avenue school, shown here in 1913, had curious Byzantine towers with cupolas at each end. The building is dated 1902 on the front.

32. Looking just like a fortress, Napier Road school had many good facilities inside, making it an improvement on many Victorian inner-city buildings. Note the number of chimneys. Two masters are on hand to control the few children allowed to pose for the camera. The date on the front, a feature of many East Ham buildings, is 1901, but *Kelly's Directory* says the school was built in 1902 to accommodate 568 boys, 568 girls and 530 infants.

33. An early picture of Kensington Avenue schools. A number of children are formed up in the playground, some in ranks and some in a large circle, arranged alternately girl/boy/girl. All the girls wear pinafores and some of the boys sailor suits.

34. This 1906 view of Manor Park school shows the girls' and infants' entrances in the foreground. The message on the back of the card reads: 'I wish I were at this school instead of at Kensington Avenue'.

35. Members and masters of the Plashet Lane Football Club for the 1925-6 season; a keen-looking group of players, smartly turned out.

36a & b. The Technical Institute, afterwards the Technical College, was East Ham's pride and joy – a pioneer in developing trade and scientific courses. It was opened by the Prince and Princess of Wales on 18 March 1905.

37a & b. The North Woolwich Gardens, once a rather remote attraction, became notorious in the later 19th century and were closed due to their bad reputation. They later re-opened as the Royal Victoria Gardens, and became a place for a sedate promenade on the banks of the Thames.

38. Another remarkably commendable municipal endeavour was the provision of public libraries in the district. Now people who had had difficulties whilst at school could pursue education independently or remedy the deficiencies of their school syllabus. Self education benefited many. Plashet library was the second library in the district, a converted house in North Woolwich being the first. The benefactor, J. Passmore Edwards, contributed towards the cost.

39. Manor Park library seen here in 1912. This was the first of the Carnegie Trust donated buildings in East Ham and cost £5,000. Opened in 1905, the ground floor consisted of a lending library, newspaper room and magazine room. The first floor comprised a spacious lecture hall accommodating 200 and available to hire for lectures, concerts and public meetings. By 1930 the lending library contained 18,280 volumes, making 189, 993 issues in that year.

40. The entrance to the Central library, a second Carnegie library, which opened in 1908. This contained a link with the past – a bust of Mrs. Elizabeth Fry, the prison philanthropist, who lived at Plashet House between 1809-29. The reference section of the library could hold 5,300 volumes and was furnished with 24 chairs and 12 double-sided tables for students.

41a. Two of the area's hospitals. The Passmore Edwards Hospital in Shrewsbury Road is shown here in 1918 when it was being used for treating soldiers wounded in the war.

41b. Queen Mary at the Memorial Hospital, 24 July 1929. The hospital was built as a memorial to the 2,000 East Ham men killed in the First World War. It contained 100 beds, operating theatre, x-ray department, massage department and outpatients section. This was a great improvement on the 20 beds and modest facilities of the old cottage hospital.

42a. In the period leading up to the First World War tremendous efforts were made to raise money for the hospitals through carnivals and similar events. The hospital carnival was an important social event and many of East Ham's population were involved in either riding on the floats, or else preparing for the great day. Here the floats and decorated bikes are being judged before they move off in procession.

42b. G. H. Vandy's float portrays a domestic scene to amuse the spectators in the humour section of the competition.

42c. A policeman casts a benevolent eye over the children of Hartley Avenue on their *Midsummer Night's Dream* float. By 1907 the standard of presentation was quite high and judging proved difficult.

42d. The procession passing down the High Street. The tram has come to a stop whilst the parade passes.

43. The municipal road sweeper – a vital link in a chain of good order and cleanliness.

Civic Pride: Transport

44. The *Coach and Horses* was a busy coaching inn on the Essex Road. In the early years of the 19th century it was hard for people connected with the coaching trade to foresee that anything would alter, as they had years of prosperity behind them. They were not to know that railways would suddenly appear challenging their supremacy.

45a & b. Both the old Essex Road to the north and the Barking Road to the south had turnpikes for collection of road toll charges. Unfortunately few photographs of these exist. The picture on the left shows the remains of Little Ilford turnpike, and the picture on the right shows the Barking Road tollbooth complete with rails and gates.

46. This picture shows the *Duke's Head*, a real traveller's public house, on the Barking Road, with patrons taking their refreshment.

47. The London, Tilbury and Southend Railway opened the cut-off line from Bromley and Plaistow to East Ham and Barking on 31 March 1858. Before this L.T.S.R. trains had run via Stratford and Forest Gate down to Barking and Tilbury. East Ham now had a station of its own and a primitive shelter on the down line, shown here about 1888.

48. This picture from the 1890s shows commuters and onlookers watching the photographer from the High Street as he takes a shot of the rickety steps leading down to the platform. The wooden cabin on the left may be for the sale of newspapers and refreshments.

49. A view of the platform, staff and platform building in the 1890s. A fire appears to have damaged the roof of the building.

50. The station flourished and an entrance hall was built on a bridge, which gave access to all platforms. Excursions to places all over the country were run from here and Southend trippers often changed here en route from North London via the Tottenham and Hampstead line. In this picture the aggressive L.M.S.R. excursion advertising billboards can be clearly seen. The East Ham Palace variety theatre, next to the station, brought its own share of rail traffic to add to that generated by High Street North's excellent shopping facilities.

51. Tracklaying for East Ham Corporation tramways at Boleyn Castle, Green Street. The first trams were run by the Corporation on 22 June 1901. The tram depot was in Nelson Street, behind the Town Hall.

52. Inside the depot with an early open-top car being inspected following delivery. In 1900 East Ham councillors visited Liverpool in order to see what they could learn from the local authorities about tramway operation.

53a & b. Trams soon became an accepted part of the scenery on their designated routes, and parts of some routes were not without their sylvan charm. Trams are seen here *(above)* at the junction of Romford Road and Green Street and *(below)* Plashet Grove in the mid-1900s. Presumably the trees were cut back soon after this photograph was taken. Note the unconcerned walkers following the tram.

54. A more urban scene in Plashet Lane with open and covered top cars and a number of shops.

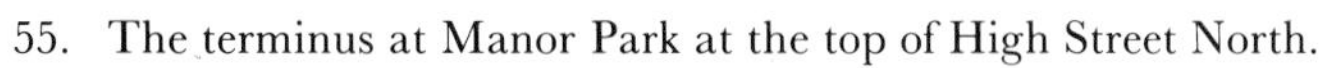

55. The terminus at Manor Park at the top of High Street North.

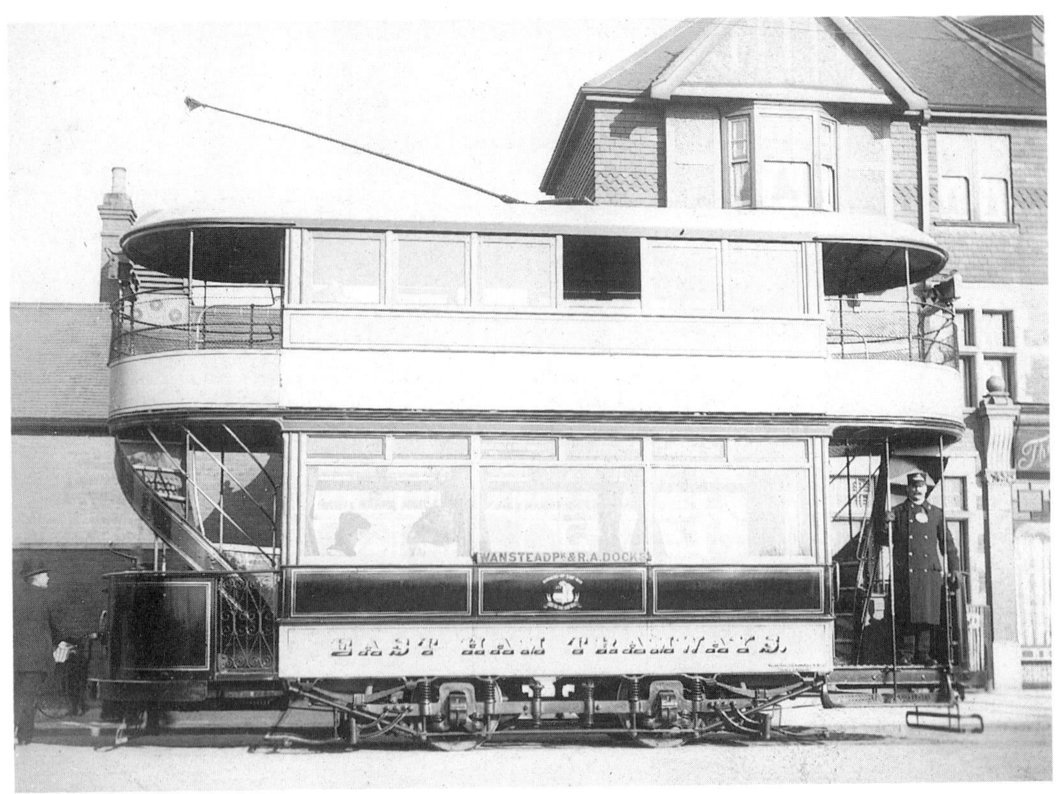

56. A smartly dressed tram driver poses with his vehicle, a new four-wheel car with covered top, on the north to south Wanstead Park and Royal Albert Dock route.

57. An East Ham car at Stratford, with a West Ham car behind.

58. A list of tramway fares from 1931. In 1917 the range had been from ½d. for the first group of journeys to 2½d. for the final group.

BOROUGH TRAMWAY ROUTES AND FARES

All parts of the borough are quickly accessible by means of the Borough Tramways, which provide a service at frequent intervals on each route. The following are the routes and the fares :

1.	Wanstead Park to Ruskin Avenue	1d.
2.	Manor Park Station to East Ham Station	
3.	Ruskin Avenue to East Ham Town Hall	
4.	East Ham Station to Charlemont Road	
5.	East Ham Town Hall to Beckton Road	
6.	Charlemont Road to Royal Albert Docks	
1.	Wanstead Park to East Ham Station	1½d.
2.	Manor Park Station to East Ham Town Hall	
3.	Ruskin Avenue to Charlemont Road	
4.	East Ham Station to Beckton Road	
5.	East Ham Town Hall to Royal Albert Docks	
1.	Wanstead Park to East Ham Town Hall	2d.
2.	Manor Park Station to Charlemont Road	
3.	Ruskin Avenue to Beckton Road	
4.	East Ham Station to Royal Albert Docks	
1.	Wanstead Park to Charlemont Road	2½d.
2.	Manor Park Station to Beckton Road	
3.	Ruskin Avenue to Royal Albert Docks	
1.	Wanstead Park to Beckton Road	3d.
2.	Manor Park Station to Royal Albert Docks	
1.	Wanstead Park to Royal Albert Docks	3½d.

Through running is in force from Aldgate to Ilford Broadway and to Barking Broadway ; also from High Street, East Ham, to Stratford Broadway (via Plashet Grove).

59. A foggy day with a crew waiting at Wanstead Flats terminus.

60a. Several roads overlooking Wanstead Flats came within the East Ham boundaries and had ready access to the open space provided by the Flats. Capel Road, shown above, is a good example.

60b. The Flats provided a fine promenade and fresh air for the inhabitants of the crowded streets to the south and west.

61. Three transport related advertisements.
(right) An old fashioned removal wagon, 1917.
(below left) An early Ford dealer's advertisement aimed at tradesmen, 1917.
(below right) Edwards and Newman coach booking office, 1931.

132-134, Barking Road, East Ham,
And 93, ILFORD LANE.

EXPERIENCED WORKMEN ONLY. PERSONAL SUPERVISION.
HOME AND FOREIGN REMOVALS.
Lino taken up and relaid the day before.
Furniture Repaired, Re-Polished and Re-Upholstered. Carpets taken up, Beaten Shampooed and Relaid. All kinds of Bedding Re-made.
Telephones—East Ham 263 and Ilford 737.

THE PROGRESSIVE TRADESMAN who wants to extend his business has a powerful ally in a FORD CAR.

1. **To begin with, it is low-priced, yet made of the best materials, and with ordinary care will last for years.**
2. **It saves time and money. It covers the ground at a minimum of expense and is a strong advertisement both for your goods and your enterprise.**
3. **Spare parts are always in stock—no waiting or extravagant prices for minor repairs or renewals.**

20 H.P. Efficiently equipped—Steel Panelled Body with double doors at rear. Extreme height, floor to roof, 52 in.; extreme width, 51 in.; length behind driver, 50 in.; width of well, 35 in. Price (at Works, Manchester), **£130.** For fuller particulars and demonstration apply to—

Ranson & Edwards Ltd.

"THREE RABBITS" YARD,
MANOR PARK, LONDON, E.
'Phone No. 711 Ilford.

We specialise in every kind of Ford Service—Repairs, Body-work, Painting, Upholstering, etc. We adapt the van to your needs.

EDWARDS & NEWMAN Leading Local Booking Agency
6 HIGH STREET NORTH, EAST HAM, E.6
Telephone—Grangewood 1075, 1076

62. The Ferry Approach, North Woolwich, offered two ways of crossing the Thames. The free ferry waited at the pontoon behind the bus, whilst the foot tunnel could be entered via the round building to be seen on the right. An ice-cream vendor plys his trade by the footpath. This picture dates from 1913.

63. The ferryboat, *Hutton* mid-stream, 1911.

64. At the end of the foot tunnel pedestrians had the choice of climbing the stairs or going in a lift. This photograph dates from 1913.

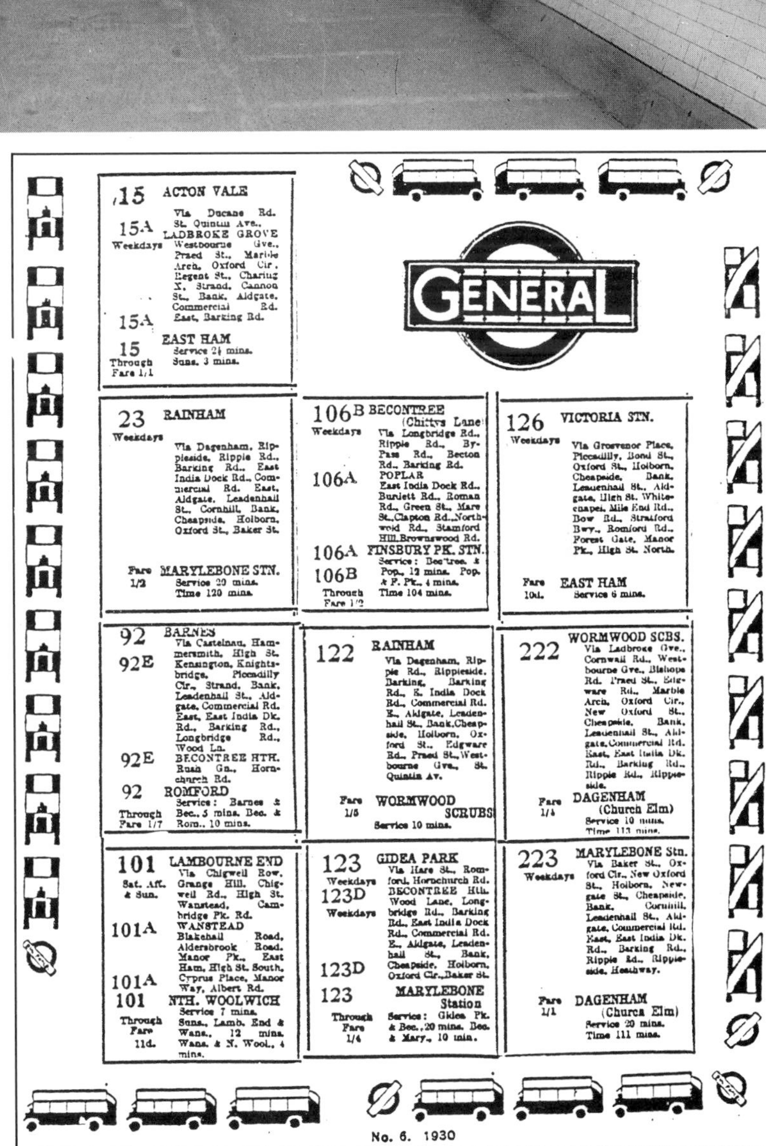

GENERAL

15 ACTON VALE
15A
Weekdays
Via Ducane Rd. St. Quintin Ave., LADBROKE GROVE Westbourne Gve., Praed St., Marble Arch, Oxford Cir., Regent St., Charing X, Strand, Cannon St., Bank, Aldgate, Commercial Rd. East, Barking Rd.
15A
15 EAST HAM
Service 2½ mins. Suns. 3 mins.
Through Fare 1/1

23 RAINHAM
Weekdays
Via Dagenham, Rippleside, Ripple Rd., Barking Rd., East India Dock Rd., Commercial Rd. East, Aldgate, Leadenhall St., Cornhill, Bank, Cheapside, Holborn, Oxford St., Baker St.
Fare 1/2 MARYLEBONE STN.
Service 20 mins. Time 120 mins.

106B BECONTREE (Chittys Lane)
Weekdays
Via Longbridge Rd., Ripple Rd., By-Pass Rd., Becton Rd., Barking Rd.
106A POPLAR
East India Dock Rd., Burdett Rd., Roman Rd., Green St., Mare St., Clapton Rd., Northwold Rd., Stamford Hill, Brownswood Rd.
106A FINSBURY PK. STN.
106B
Service: Bec'tree. & Pop., 12 mins. Pop. & F. Pk., 4 mins.
Time 104 mins.
Through Fare 1/2

126 VICTORIA STN.
Weekdays
Via Grosvenor Place, Piccadilly, Bond St., Oxford St., Holborn, Cheapside, Bank, Leadenhall St., Aldgate, High St. Whitechapel, Mile End Rd., Bow Rd., Stratford Bwy., Romford Rd., Forest Gate, Manor Pk., High St. North.
Fare 10d. EAST HAM
Service 6 mins.

92 BARNES
92E
Via Castelnau, Hammersmith, High St. Kensington, Knightsbridge, Piccadilly Cir., Strand, Bank, Leadenhall St., Aldgate, Commercial Rd. East, East India Dk. Rd., Barking Rd., Longbridge Rd., Wood Ln.
92E BECONTREE HTH.
Rush Gn., Hornchurch Rd.
92 ROMFORD
Service: Barnes & Bec., 5 mins. Bec. & Rom., 10 mins.
Through Fare 1/7

122 RAINHAM
Via Dagenham, Ripple Rd., Rippleside, Barking, Barking Rd., E. India Dock Rd., Commercial Rd. E., Aldgate, Leadenhall St., Bank, Cheapside, Holborn, Oxford St., Edgware Rd., Praed St., Westbourne Gve., St. Quintin Av.
Fare 1/5 WORMWOOD SCRUBS
Service 10 mins.

222 WORMWOOD SCBS.
Via Ladbroke Gve., Cornwall Rd., Westbourne Gve., Bishops Rd. Praed St., Edgware Rd., Marble Arch, Oxford Cir., New Oxford St., Cheapside, Bank, Leadenhall St., Aldgate, Commercial Rd. East, East India Dk. Rd., Barking Rd., Ripple Rd., Rippleside.
Fare 1/4 DAGENHAM (Church Elm)
Service 10 mins. Time 113 mins.

101 LAMBOURNE END
Sat. Aft. & Sun.
Via Chigwell Row, Grange Hill, Chigwell Rd., High St. Wanstead, Cambridge Pk. Rd.
101A WANSTEAD
Blakehall Road, Aldersbrook Road, Manor Pk., East Ham, High St. South, Cyprus Place, Manor Way, Albert Rd.
101A
101 NTH. WOOLWICH
Service 7 mins. Suns., Lamb. End & Wans., 12 mins. Wans. & N. Wool., 4 mins.
Through Fare 11d.

123 GIDEA PARK
Weekdays
Via Hare St., Romford, Hornchurch Rd.
123D BECONTREE Hth.
Weekdays
Wood Lane, Longbridge Rd., Barking Rd., East India Dock Rd., Commercial Rd. E., Aldgate, Leadenhall St., Bank, Cheapside, Holborn, Oxford Cir., Baker St.
123D
123 MARYLEBONE Station
Service: Gidea Pk. & Bec., 20 mins. Bec. & Mary., 10 min.
Through Fare 1/4

223 MARYLEBONE Stn.
Weekdays
Via Baker St., Oxford Cir., New Oxford St., Holborn, Newgate St., Cheapside, Bank, Cornhill, Leadenhall St., Aldgate, Commercial Rd. East, East India Dk. Rd., Barking Rd., Ripple Rd., Rippleside, Heathway.
Fare 1/1 DAGENHAM (Church Elm)
Service 20 mins. Time 111 mins.

No. 6. 1930

65. Travelling by bus, 1930. Details of routes and times.

66. This picture of 1933 shows an open-stair bus on route 101 waiting in High Street South. The London Transport Board had only recently been formed at this time.

67. The docks have been reached by bus 101, but a large Atlantic Transport Line steamship has caused a traffic jam while she passes through. Such an event gave the name of a 'bridger' to the ship involved. There was little the assembled traffic could do but remain patient and enjoy the sight.

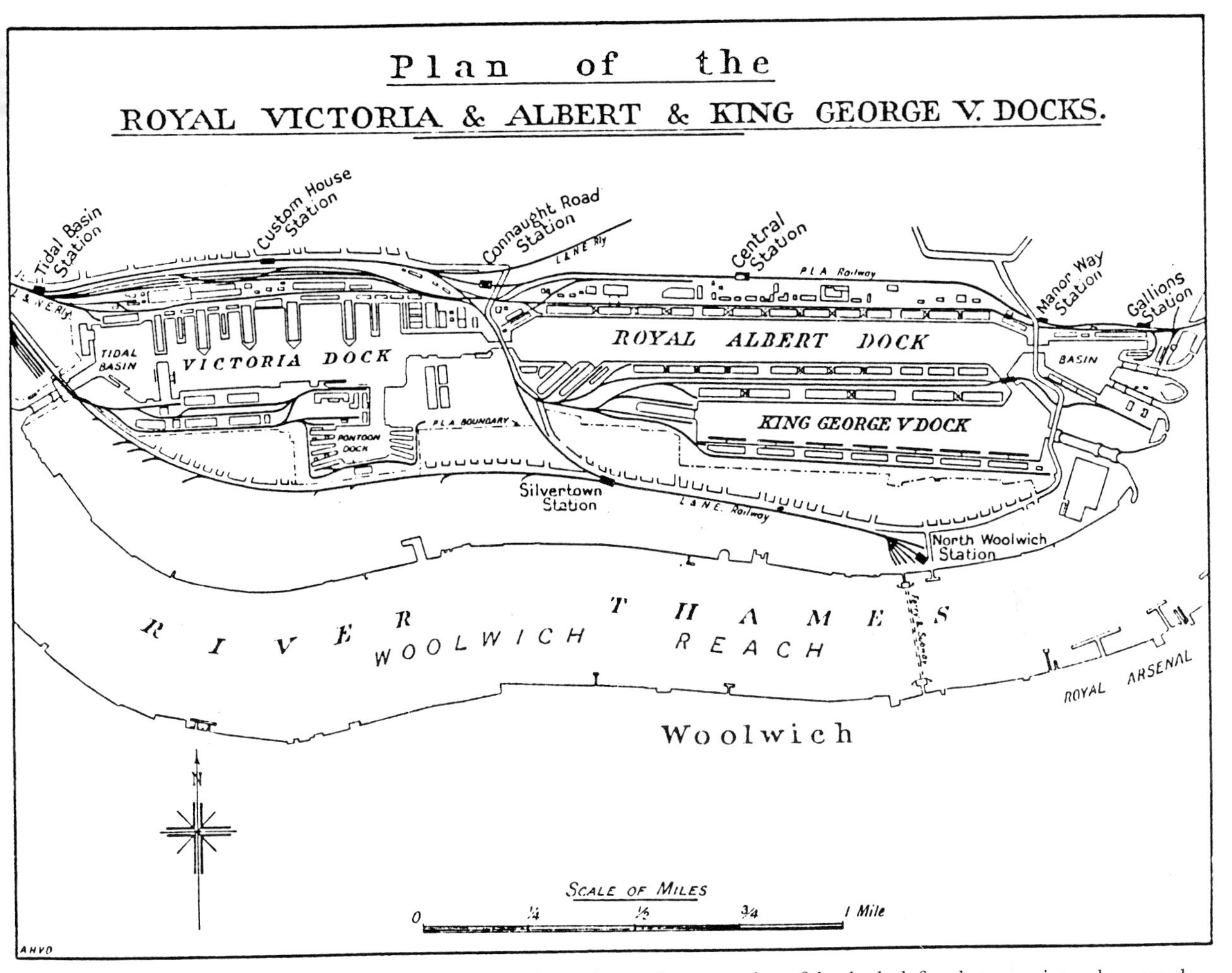

68. The completed plan of the Royal Docks. As has been shown the expansion of the docks left only two points where roads could exit and enter from the Thames bank.

69. The Royal Victoria and Albert Docks were officially opened by the Duke and Duchess of Connaught in 1880. The Victoria Dock was in West Ham, but a large part of the Albert Dock fell within the East Ham boundary.

70. Running down from High Street South to the docks, Manor Way passed through this little settlement, curiously named Cyprus, with its own shops. In many ways this Port of London Authority owned area was a self-supporting community.

71. Dockside and transit sheds in the Royal Albert Dock, 1904.

72. Policemen on duty in the Royal Albert Dock during the 1912 dock strike. During the strike all leave was cancelled, and due to the long working hours, many men did not see their children awake for weeks on end.

73. In the lock, Royal Albert Dock, 1906.

74. Interior of a transit shed, 1926.

75. This photograph of the Royal Albert export berths was taken after the Second World War and shows to what extent the docks were mechanised.

76. This banner was displayed at the opening of the George V Dock in 1921. It was erected by the unemployed in order to draw attention to their plight.

77. *(left)* The massive lock gates at the George V Dock in 1926.

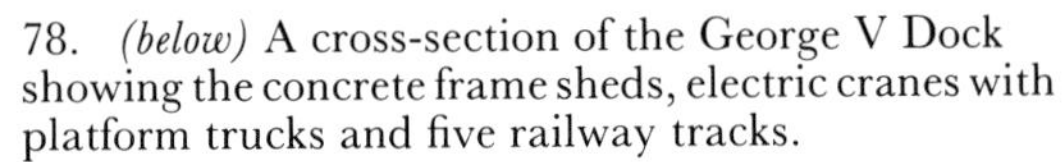

78. *(below)* A cross-section of the George V Dock showing the concrete frame sheds, electric cranes with platform trucks and five railway tracks.

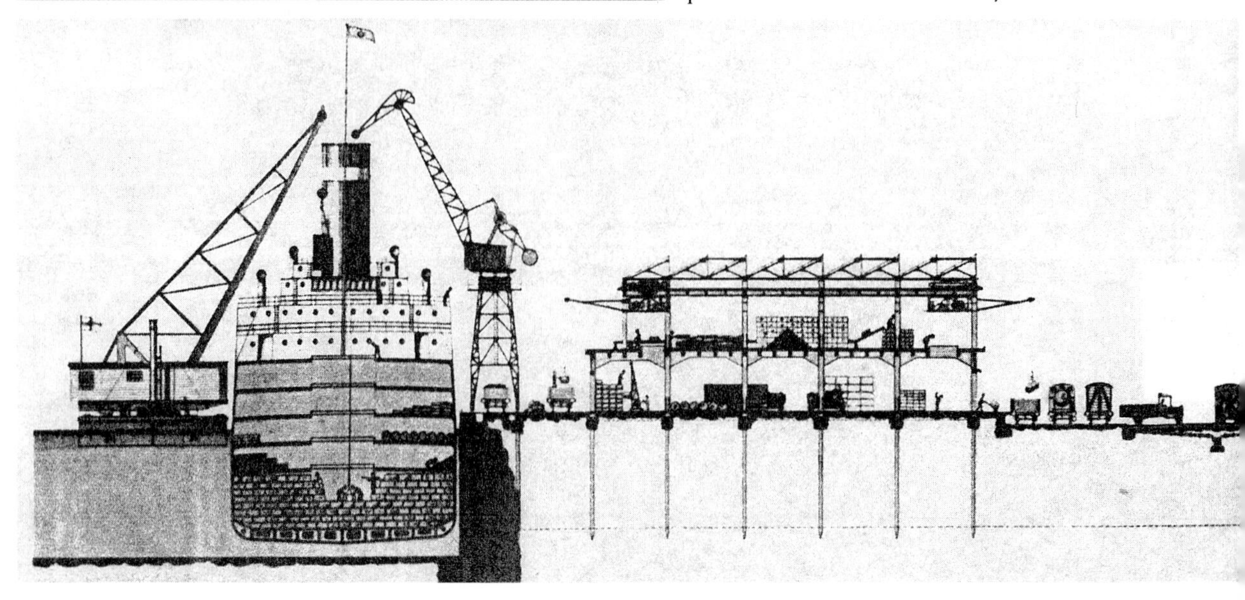

79. The Blue Star Liner, *Almeda*, passes through the George V entrance lock after her maiden voyage, 6 April 1927.

80. An artist's impression of the *Maraunoa's* entry into the lock showing the process of 'warping', whereby a large ships are drawn into dock using cables, the narrow clearances preventing the use of engines.

81. Aerial views of the Royal docks.

2. A tug assists a ship through a lock in the 1940s.

3. Workers stream off a North Woolwich-bound rolleybus, which has just come over the bridge into ockland. This picture dates from the 1950s.

84. George V Dock. The photographer has composed a memorable vista of ships, cranes and warehouses with a glimpse of the vastness beyond.

85. A scene in the Geoge V Dock. Goods could be trans-shipped from the ships in the background across to barges in the channel in the foreground.

West Ham United – Kings of Boleyn Castle

One of the contributing factors to the glamour of many league football teams is the knowledge that they have survived all their early vicissitudes, often including near extinction, but nevertheless have survived to become famous. The story of West Ham bears this out, for the early years of the team were spent playing on various grounds, and having lost their ground they were offered the opportunity of moving to their present venue – the Boleyn ground, which stands just inside the boundaries of East Ham. The name comes from the romantic myth that Henry VIII and Anne Boleyn made their early trysts on this site, in the grounds of the Green Street House, close by Boleyn Tower. The tower, a detached part of the property, stood until comparatively recently. It formed a notable landmark behind its ancient brick wall alongside the southern limits of Green Street. When West Ham moved to the Boleyn ground, one passageway into the club actually passed by the tower, on the inside of the wall.

The West Ham club owed its origin to enthusiasts within Thames Ironworks Limited, who came together to form an amateur team, which played initially on the Hermit Road 'cinder heap', as it was described at the time. The Hermit Road site had only been vacated since 1895 following the demise of the Old Castle Swifts club, a club distinguished by being the first professional soccer club in Essex.

On 7 September 1895, 11 men from the ironworks turned out at Hermit Road and played the reserve team from the Royal Ordnance F.C., the result a draw. It should be mentioned that Thames Ironworks was involved in building warships on the banks of the Thames and many of the platers and riveters employed had come down to London from the north, where they had been enthusiastic football supporters. Add to this ardour the fact the local area was a hotbed of football, many good teams such as St Luke's, St Luke's Old Boys and the Old Castle Swifts being supported and it can be seen that there was a great deal of backing behind the team. However, support did not guarantee a club's survival and the first captain of the T.I.W. squad, 'Bob' Stevenson (he also captained Woolwich Arsenal at one point) and the trainer, Tommy Robinson, made sure that some hard training was done, during the week at a schoolroom on the Barking Road and on moonlit nights on runs along the turnpike road. By the end of their first season the team had had some good results. The following year, however, they had to move from Hermit Road to Browning Road, East Ham. For some reason, difficult to fathom, the local public did not take kindly to the team and records show that Browning Road was a desert, both in the matter of luck and support. Those nearest the club still believed that they had a bright future and supporters began to raise their sights on the Memorial Grounds at Canning Town, a vast athletic complex built by Mr. Hills and opened in 1897. Moving to this venue still did not provide the club with the support it deserved, but they nevertheless won the London League Championship in 1898. The following season they entered the

Second Division of the Southern League and, unbelievably, won the championship. During the 1898-9 season the club turned professional. In September 1899 they entered the Southern League's First Division and immediately found the competition much tougher; they were only able to win eight matches, finishing just above Sheppey United.

In spite of setbacks on the field the team was gaining public interest and support and the officials decided that it was time that the team became a limited liability company, and the public was soon invited to take up shares. In 1900 the club's name was changed from Thames Ironworks to West Ham United. Players were now obtained from other clubs, but much of the talent was home-grown and the following year the club finished sixth in the Southern League.

Even the reserve team was bursting with talent at this time, several players coming through to play for other famous clubs later in the century, players such as J. Bigden (Arsenal) and Yenson (Queens Park Rangers). West Ham made consistent progress until the arrival of the 1902-3 season. At the start of the year it was known that the agreement for the occupancy of the Memorial Ground had to be re-negotiated. The directors failed to negotiate satisfactorily with A. F. Hills for a continuance of the lease for 7, 14 or 21 years at a reasonable rent and the club having sole control. This led to impasse by the end of 1904. During the last few days at the Memorial Ground the club's future looked bleak. During those last few days a match was being played between boys from two Home Office schools, one of the Catholic brothers from the Boleyn Castle school was a spectator along with officials from West Ham. In conversation the Club's problems were revealed and out of the blue an arrangement was made for the officials to go and see the Boleyn Castle field, which had been a cabbage patch. West Ham agreed to take the field, but were thrown into despair when they heard that the Home Office disapproved of the brothers' action. Officials lobbied the M.P., Sir Ernest Gray, and eventually, suject to certain conditions, the ground was allowed to pass to the West Ham club. The decision was momentous as the stability provided by this well-placed arena seemed to encourage the team towards success.

During the First World War, London clubs played in a Combination League, in order to compensate for their own players' absence due to the war. West Ham was to field many guest players, stationed or passing through London. Some exciting displays of football were seen as the team played with leading players, such as Sam Chedgzoy, George Harrison and J. Macconicle (Everton), Andrew Cunningham (Rangers), Percy Smith (Blackburn), Roberts (Preston North End), McDougal (Liverpool) and Brownlie (Third Lanark).

Having experienced the delights of such classic football, as soon as the League Programme resumed in 1919-20 the club applied to and were elected to Division Two of the Football League. Their performances became increasingly impressive and during the next four seasons they finished seventh, fifth, fourth and finally, in 1922-23, second. Not only had they clinched promotion to Division One but, in the most successful season in their history, the club actually won through to the F.A. Cup Final. The pictures of this memorable final, the first to be played at Wembley, show a tumultuous occasion where the crowd broke into the unfinished stadium and thronged the pitch. Although a policeman on a white horse saved the day by driving the crowd back peacably, football rules were broken in allowing the final to proceed whilst the fans were still yards over the touchlines all round the pitch. Although beaten on this occasion by Bolton Wanderers, the 'Hammers' were destined to return in later years to win.

The nickname of 'Hammers' comes as much from the shipbuilding tools displayed on their badge as from the fact the team comes from East Ham, an earlier rallying cry was 'Up the Irons'. From their first outstanding season onwards, West Ham took part in many Continental tours, playing in Austria, Germany, Hungary, France, Spain, Holland, Denmark, Sweden, Norway, Switzerland and Czechoslavakia.

In January 1913 the team was involved in, a sensational transfer, Danny Shea going to Blackburn for the record sum of £2,000; later in 1921 Syd Puddefoot went to Falkirk for another record fee of £5,000. Early players who graduated from the Club becoming England Internationals included Jimmy Barrett, Len Goulden, Ted Hufton, Syd Puddefoot, Jimmy Ruffell, Jack Tresadern, George Webb, V .M. Watson, W. Brown, S. G. J. Earle, W. Moore, J. Morton and W. Williams.

West Ham were early pioneers of playing under electric lights. The lights were mounted on poles at the Hermit Road ground for matches against Arsenal and West Bromwich Albion in 1896.

86. This picture shows Green Street House and Boleyn Castle whilst it was still being used as a Catholic reformatory school. The tradition that Henry VIII visited Ann Boleyn here is erroneous. The building, which was erected about 1550, was a good example of Tudor brickwork construction. Rebuilding took place in the late 17th century.

87. The Boleyn Castle tower with its battlemented parapet and stair turret may be seen overlooking Green Street. Army recruitment posters are fixed to the wall. The picture dates from about 1912.

88. Details of the early 17th-century staircase and the roof construction of Boleyn Castle.

89. In 1904 West Ham football club bought land from the Catholic authorities and laid out a new ground, having been unable to renegotiate the lease on their old site. Only the tower was owned and used by the club, the main house and grounds remaining in the hands of the Catholic authorities, therefore the path into this part of the ground followed a circuitous route, behind the wall facing Green Street. For some time the club used the tower as a social club.

90. Entrance to the West Ham football club ground, *c.*1919. The banking on this Castle Street side is not covered.

91. This picture, which dates from 1904-5, shows the ground after it had first been laid out.

92. The West Ham team in 1905-6. Having resolved the problem of obtaining a permanent home, the club could look forward to a bright future. The chairman at this time was J. Grisdale.

93. The team won through to the F.A. Cup Final in 1923, the first to be played in the nearly finished Wembley Stadium. There were no reserved tickets and this is what happened inside the ground – the pitch was completely overwhelmed by spectators who managed to gain access.

94. The match, which was against the famous northern club, Bolton Wanderers, went ahead even though the pitch was not clear. Here we see Kay and Brown of West Ham in a heading duel with Seddon of Bolton. In the centre behind is David Jack, scorer of the first goal at Wembley. The game finished with the Hammers losing 2-0, but, according to the rules, which stated that the pitch should be clear, it probably should have been replayed.

95. Some of the crowd have been cleared by a policeman on a white horse, but others remain.

96. A West Ham attack in the 1923 final. Moore (centre) receives a pass from Ruffell. After the Second World War another Moore captained England to victory in the 1966 World Cup. Two other West Ham players, Hurst and Peters, were in the same squad. West Ham also won the F.A. Cup and the European Cup Winners Cup. Bobby Moore was idolised by his fans and in 1993 following his premature death a memorial was placed at the main gates of the West Ham ground surrounded with flowers and tributes.

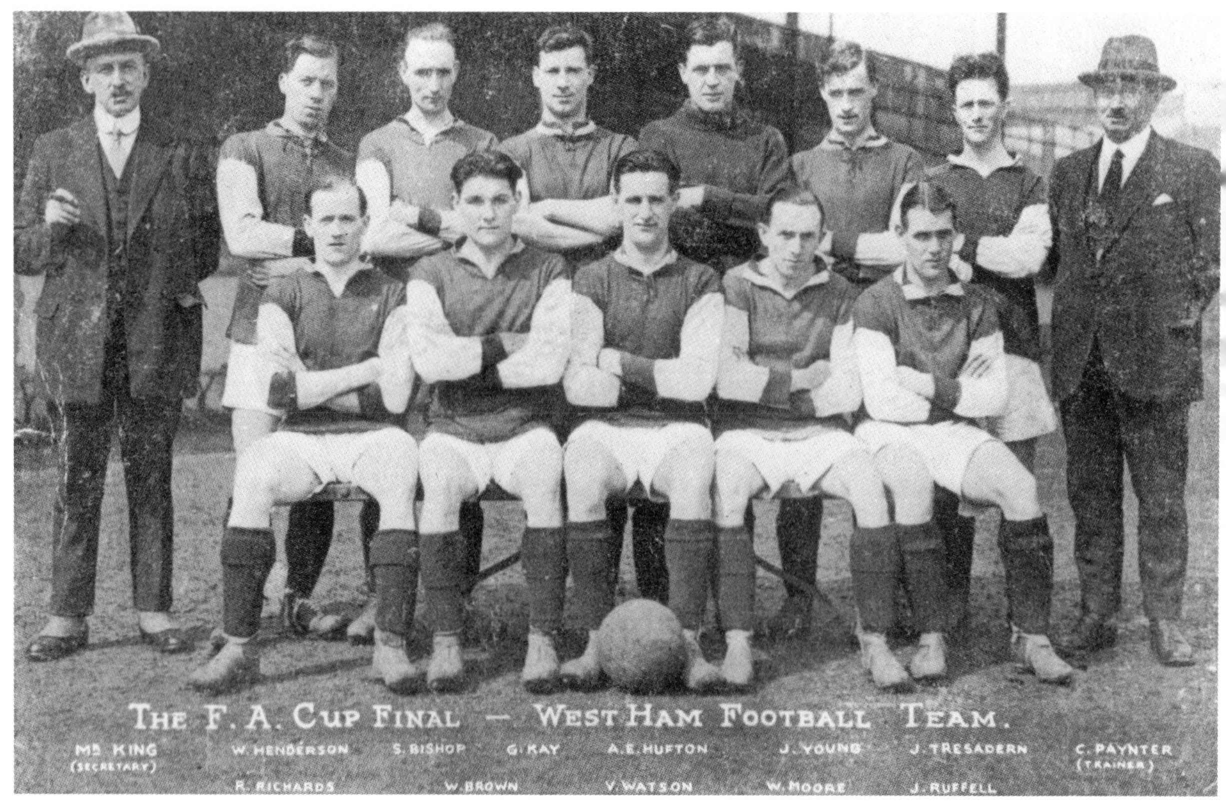

97. The players who took West Ham to their first Cup Final and gained promotion in 1923.

98a. Men of Iron. Charlie Paynter and Syd King, 1923. Both joined West Ham as players in 1900. King stayed on as secretary-manager betweeen 1901-32. Paynter became assistant trainer from 1902, trainer 1912, team manager 1932, and then secretary manager until after the Second World War. Paynter's career with the club spanned almost fifty years. West Ham have only had seven managers since they were formed.

98b. *(far left)* West Ham born Syd Puddefoot takes a kick – he was a courageous, tough forward. Falkirk surprised everybody by paying the first £5,000 transfer fee for him. He later gained two England caps.

98c. *(left)* Len Goulden, another England international and West Ham favourite, poses proudly in the club colours.

99. The original 'Chicken Run' stand; this has now been replaced but the name survives.

A Local Hero, East Ham and the First World War

During the Battle of Jutland, in May 1916 East Ham added to its prestige by gaining a V.C. and a national hero. John Cornwell, a lad from Manor Park, was only 16 when he took part in the battle aboard H.M.S. *Chester*. Admiral Beatty mentioned him in a memorable dispatch:

> A report from the Commanding Officer of *Chester* gives a splendid instance of devotion to duty. Boy (1st Class) John Travers Cornwell was mortally wounded early in the action. He nevertheless remained standing alone at a most exposed post, quietly awaiting orders till the end of the action, with the gun's crew dead and wounded round him. His age was under 16½ years. I regret that he has since died, but I recommend his case for special recognition in justice to his memory and as an acknowledgement of the high example set by him.

Some background to the story is provided by a biography written at the time.

> If you had been standing on the platform of a certain London station on 14 October 1915, you might have noticed a group of a dozen or so boys. The eldest was about eighteen, the youngest was just under sixteen, and his name was Jack Travers Cornwell. Although he and his companions were still dressed in ordinary clothes (their Sunday best, I fancy) they were actually on that day all members of His Majesty's Navy. Only a little time before these boys had been at school, or selling newspapers in the street, calling out the latest news of the war, or acting as messengers – in some way or another trying to do the work of men who had gone to war. But now they were 'Boys -2nd Class' entitled to draw pay at the rate of sixpence a week and 'all found', which means that they were to be fed and clothed at the cost of the country.

Jack Cornwell, as he was always called, was the second son of a happy family which included three boys and a girl. His mother and father were both country folk, one coming from Cambridgeshire, the other from Bedfordshire. There had never been much money to spend in their home at Manor Park, and it had not been easy to make ends meet since war had broken out, for the father, a retired soldier and long past military age, had re-joined the army when he heard Kitchener's call for more men. Although Jack Cornwell had few advantages, leaving school when he was 14, he had a patriot for a father, and that's a very big advantage indeed. His mother, too, was always full of cheerful courage, working to keep things going whilst her husband was away. She was helped by her eldest son, who worked at a factory and by Jack, who upon leaving school got a job as a delivery boy on one of Brooke Bond's tea vans.

Jack had always wanted to be a sailor. He had watched the vessels setting out from the Thames or steaming into dock laden with treasure from distant lands. As a schoolboy he had listened eagerly to tales told by 'old boys' who returned to visit classmates when on leave from the Navy; his school had sent many boys into the Navy, there being at least a dozen on the *Impregnable* alone.

There came a day when Jack Cornwell made up his mind to join up; 'Your Country Needs You' he read on a hundred posters. He went to the recruiting office and asked if he could serve in the Navy. He took with him letters from his headmaster and employer as references. His character was excellent. Yes, his country needed him. Jack Cornwell was just an ordinary boy; no one spoke of him as especially clever or ambitious. He was quiet and reserved, seldom gave any trouble and was always straight and truthful. One of his teachers summed him up by saying, 'We always felt we could depend upon him'.

When the battle was over and the wounded were carried below decks, the doctors saw that little could be done for Jack. As soon as possible he was taken ashore and placed in a Grimsby hospital. He could still speak a little and, although in great pain, he remained quietly cheerful. The matron asked him how the battle had gone and he replied, 'Oh, we carried on alright'. These were almost his last words. His mother, having received a telegram from the Admiralty, was on her way to her son. She failed to arrive in time, but just before he died Jack said, 'Give mother my love. I know she is coming'.

In the September following his tragic death, the king approved the granting of a Victoria Cross to the hero. A splendid funeral took place in Manor Park cemetery. In attendance were Dr. J. T. Macnamara (representing the Admiralty), Sir John Bethell, M.P. for Romford (his constituency included East Ham, but he and his wife were also great benefactors of East Ham), representatives of the Navy League, the Mayor, Councillors and Town Clerk of East Ham, the Bishop of Barking and many other dignitaries. The bishop and Dr. Macnamara made speeches at the graveside. The bishop then pronounced the benediction, three volleys were discharged by the firing party and the Last Post was sounded. This moving ceremony concluded with the placing of a floral anchor on the grave by shipmates of the deceased and a wreath by half a dozen naval cadets. East Ham honoured its own – dense crowds lined the route to the cemetery and shopkeepers suspended business whilst the cortege passed. All the funeral expenses were borne by the Admiralty. To this day the local British Legion and Sea Cadets mark the event on the appropriate day.

The Cornwell family had not completed its sacrifice on behalf of the nation. Almost a month after Jack's funeral his father was buried in the same grave, with military honours. In March 1915 Private Eli Cornwell, aged 62, had enlisted in the Essex Regiment which soon became part of the Royal Defence Corps. He died at the 57th Company camp in October of bronchial catarrh. He had previously served 14 years with the R.A.M.C., seen active service in Egypt and South Africa and possessed the Soudan medal and Khedive Star.

In common with other areas the declaration of war on 4 August 1914 changed the local scene, bringing many new institutions to East Ham. Almost immediately a great number of army personnel and bands playing patriotic tunes on the streets, posters encouraging recruits on every hoarding and the commandeering of buildings and open spaces was introduced. The town hall and the local schools were used as recruiting offices, the municipal baths and High Street school became barracks, whilst open spaces, including Wanstead Flats, provided parade grounds.

Towards the end of 1917, the authorities in charge of home defence inaugurated a new type of aerial protection for London, whih consisted of a broken line of balloons aligned around the east side of London, stretching from Edmonton in the north to North Woolwich in the south-east. Each group of three balloons was called an 'Apron'. A network of wires suspended between the three balloons constituted the protective system. Wanstead Flats was considered an advantageous position for one of these Aprons, and work on the operation started early in 1918. The personnel consisted of four officers and about 200 other ranks. Under the Defence of the Realm Act a strip of Wanstead Flats was fenced off and engineering work began. Three balloon beds had to be constructed and surrounded by wind screens, concrete foundations made for the petrol winches, tents pitched for the guards and housing arranged for 200 men. The latter task was made easier following the requisitioning of six empty, unfurnished houses in the area, four of which were in Aldersbrook Road, facing the Flats. A telephone link connected the three balloon beds with the houses and a private exchange was installed in St John's. This experimental system was largely a morale-boosting exercise. It is said to have deterred further air attacks on the capital following the Whit Monday raid in 1918 which occurred afer the balloons had recently been installed.

It is interestingto reflect on the impact of such a large camp on the social framework of the locality. How many liaisons were formed between the locals and the 'squaddies'? Did the men involved ever consider what would have happened if the Aprons had been totally successful against unsuspecting enemy aircraft? Surely the planes would have plunged down among the men on the Flats, causing many casualties to our own side.

100. Boy V.C. John Travers Cornwell in his navy uniform while attached to H.M.S. *Lancaster*.

101. The modest home of Jack Cornwell, 10 Alverstone Road, was tucked away in the side streets of Manor Park. It was destroyed by enemy action during the Second World War.

102. The Royal Navy Recruiting Office in Second Avenue, not far from Jack's home. Is the churn being unloaded for the recruiting office's use?

103. A painting showing Cornwell waiting for orders at his post as the battle commences.

104. This painting by F. Matania shows Cornwell alone at his gun post whilst all around him is devastation.

TELEPHONE ILFORD 550.

J. HAWES

Undertaker and Funeral Carriage Proprietor

Motor Hearse for long journeys.

45, STATION ROAD
MANOR PARK And at HACKNEY

105. The Cornwell family could not afford to pay for an ordinary funeral, so Jack was buried with very little ceremony. When it became known that he was to receive the Victoria Cross, the authorities decided to pay for a state funeral from national funds. Jack's body was exhumed and the local undertaker's J. Hawes made all the necessary arrangements. The coffin was carried through the streets on a gun carriage with full naval honours.

106. At Manor Park cemetery six boy seamen from H.M.S. *Chester* lay wreaths. The Bishop of Barking, T.J. Macnamara, the Financial Secretary to the Navy, the Mayor of East Ham and M.P. Sir John Bethell can be seen following the ceremony. Two gravediggers await their turn in the proceedings. The navy buglers (in the right foreground) are present to sound the Last Post.

107. The firing party fire a volley of shots as a mark of respect. Every year a ceremony is held at the graveside by the local British Legion, the Sea Cadets and dignitaries.

108. A sheet of Cornwell stamps which were sold in aid of the 'Jack Cornwell' ward at the Star and Garter Home. Stamps like these were sold in many schools. Other memorials to Jack Cornwell include the memorial houses at Hornchurch, a roll of honour in Chester cathedral, a plaque at Grimsby hospital and named beds in several other hospitals.

109. An East Ham war memorial at the corner of Alverstone Road.

110a. The first of a series of photographs of a military funeral taken by a local photographer. The body of an army hero is taken from the chapel where he has lain.

110b. The procession moves down the street, the comrades in arms marching slowly and sombrely alongside and behind the cortège.

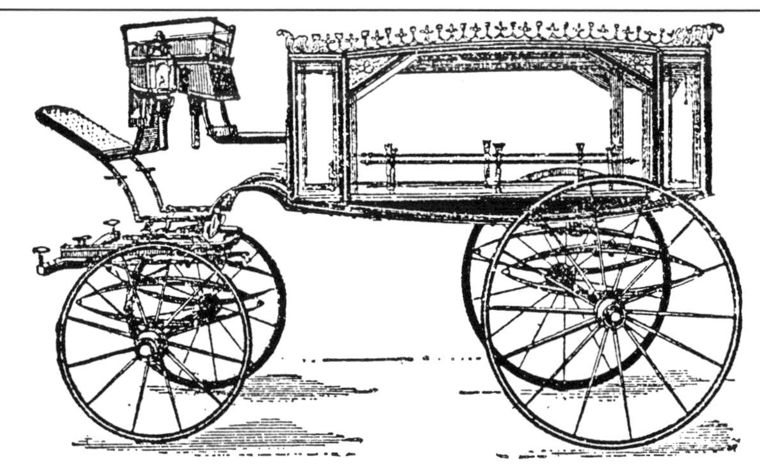

110c. An advertisement for the undertakers H. Dyer. Their services are advertised under an illustration of an older type of funeral carriage.

110d. A close-up of the underneath of the carriage as it passes a side street; it shows a typical cobbled road and a glimpse of a milk cart.

110e. The funeral procession pauses.

110f. The funeral passes under the archway of the City of London cemetery, Aldersbrook.

111. The East Ham war memorial in Central Park was designed by a local architect, R. Banks Martin. It is executed in white Portland stone with bronze tablets recording the names of over 1,600 men who fell in the war. This number brings home the scale of sacrifice made by local communities in this savage conflict.

Progress with the People: The Street Scene

112a. Two focal points of East Ham, around which traffic and commerce revolved. Bank Corner, once the site of the tollhouse, now houses the London and Provincial Bank. A crowd of onlookers, including a number of children, watch the photographer. Unusually, the road appears very quiet, with no vehicles passing to and fro.

112b. The Boleyn, as this location was known, with the suffix 'corner' taken as understood. This marked the westernmost part of the parish and borough. Here, too, the road appear very quiet. The top of the underground municipal lavatories, now a vanishing amenity, can be seen on the right.

113. The impressive looking church of St Bartholomew's. Churches such as these often organised much of the area's social life. Sunday school treats each year might provide poorer children with the best meal they would enjoy in a long time. Clubs and societies of every kind catered for family members of all ages, although the organisers were predominantly female. Outings were also organised for youngsters at little or no cost; very often these outings provided the best chance some children had of visiting the seaside or the country, in the days of large families and few state benefits.

114. Two views of the Wesleyan Central Hall, East Ham. It was conveniently placed next to the municipal buildings and provided excellent opportunities for music and worship. The exterior view shows the chimney of the East Ham electricity works. The interior photograph gives an idea of the magnificent fittings, including the grand organ.

115a. Katherine Road United Methodist church. The interior view shows the importance the church attached to music and choirs. The musical facilities offered by a church often attracted new members at a time when churches competed with each other for worshippers. The money and effort expended on new churches and their fittings to serve the new housing developments in areas such as East Ham rival the budgets that are today spent advertising consumer products in the media.

115b. An exterior view of the Methodist free church. This was one of many Christian places of worship available for the residents of East Ham. Note that the church was able to provide hall and church space for a large range of activities.

116. St Stephen's, Green Street, Upton Park seen here in 1904. The splendid church was built during the Victorian age – a period which witnessed the biggest spate of church building since the Middle Ages. The picture is full of human interest; on the left a workman carries a pack of tools slung over his shoulder, various parked and moving vehicles occupy the centre of the photograph, the newly-laid tramlines may be seen going to the right past the licensed premises of A. G. Crouch.

117. A flourishing shopping parade in Green Street during the First World War. The tramway poles may be seen on the pavement. The upstairs floors of the shops appear to be let as flats. The shop in the right foreground advertises that it is an official electrical contractor to East Ham Borough Council.

118. Green Street was one of the livelier shopping areas, due to the fact that a market was held in one section. This picture shows a little of the market-day atmosphere, with people chatting in the road, oblivious to any approaching vehicle. Shop blinds extend down the length of the road, in imitation of stall covers.

119. A genuine market scene, photographed by a camera perched on a parapet above the shops. This is obviously a summer view since the stalls in the foreground have no tarpaulins fixed over them. A projecting roofline has been used to advertise tea and there is a 'To Let' notice on the left. The advertisers seem to realise tht the throngs of shoppers visiting the market make this a good site for advertising. In 1910, before the big combines were created, there were hundreds of brands available in each product area.

120. A crowded pavement of market stalls seen from the roadway; behind them Hammerton's drapery store announces its sale. The road is so muddy that it would wreck the long skirts of any lady.

121. In Green Street market something was always about to happen, or so the various children in the foreground appear to think. They might, for instance, be rewarded for holding the reins of the carriage horse for a few moments. Note the shops of S. Fehrenbach, J. Roome and T. Cull. The Bookeries, who issued this postcard, had another shop in the main street of East Ham.

122. A photograph of Green Street taken in the 1920s. The pace of commerce has quickened, as witnessed by the great number of projecting signs. There are also more multiple stores such as the Metropolitan Boot Co. on the left. More electrical goods are being advertised and sold, for example Mazda Lamps. In the distance is a West Ham four-wheel balcony car on route 5, Canning Town to Wanstead Flats.

123. The buildings seen here, at the bottom of High Street North, have been replaced twice since this picture was taken in the mid-1900s. The church was demolished and replaced by a Co-op store, which in turn has been pulled down leaving a flat open space which today is used as car park. The *Denmark Arms*, the painted side gates of which can be seen on the left, still survives.

124. T. Cull's other shop at Cull's Corner, High Street North, can be seen on the left of this picture. Cull's was a discount bookseller and cheap stationer, still competitive at the turn of the century. David Greig's provision shop next door is an example of a multiple firm already trading in the High Street.

125. A later view of the same corner shows that a new owner, Albert Purser, has taken over the stationers whilst David Greig has an optician and dentist trading in the upper floors.

126. John Barker's corn dealers at no. 292 High Street North is located in another well-patronised length of the street. There never seems to be a shortage of children to pose for the photographer.

127. Hellens newsagents and tobacconists were situated at the top end of High Street South, and had less competition than the shops in High Street North. In the doorway of the shop is a notice advertising the firm of Pyne & Co., who are described as Scenic Artists and Stage Fitters – presumably their premises were at the rear. Perhaps they were contractors for the East Ham variety theatre? Across the road the *East Ham Echo* offices are ideally placed for following meetings at the Town Hall, for it is only a few yards up the road.

128. On the corner of Second Avenue, Manor Park, the Reliable Clothing Stores have filled their windows with so much stock that it is surely not possible to cram another item into the space.

129. The Edwardian splendour of Mark Liell's premises on the corner of High Street and Bendish Road would be the destination of a serious seeker after local property, although some might be intimidated by the art nouveau ironwork railings. These presumably went for scrap in the Second World War if they had not been dismantled before.

130. Filby Brothers of no. 832 Romford Road, Manor Park, was a typical bakery of the early part of this century. No particular attempt has been made to display the goods effectively, which have merely been placed on the shelves in the window just as they came from the bakehouse.

131. This view of 1919 shows Clover's bakery and post office with its array of delivery vehicles from the first-class site on Wanstead Park Avenue.

132. A lovely picture showing Louis Chapman newsagent's and tobacconist's at no. 139 High Street North. If the man in the shop doorway is Louis Chapman with his family they appear to be quite young, perhaps indicating that they have only recently opened or taken over the shop. In the *Kelly's Directory* of 1910 George C. Chapman is described as the owner of the shop, so perhaps Louis had taken over from his father.

133. What memories the 'new' London Co-op Departmental Stores evokes. Many local people remember the roof garden which existed at one stage. In this view, which dates from the 1930s, the shop is already proclaiming 'the Sale of the Year'. What a pity the shop has been swept away, for it certainly livened up this end of East Ham.

134. In order to show how adaptable they were, the Co-op used this building for office and warehousing. The building was the last of many versions of East Ham's manor house, Burnel Manor, to stand on this site.

135. Another venerable institution and home from home for many locals was the *White Horse* public house. The 'old' *White Horse* was certainly a few hundred years old (notice the thatched roof and chimney stacks) when it was replaced by a larger red-brick Victorian building.

The 'Cock' Hotel.

1736.

F. W. PRESS,

Proprietor.

GRAND BILLIARD SALOON

(Newly Enlarged and Decorated).

TWO NEW TABLES,

ALSO

Saloon Lounge fitted for the Comfort of Customers, Lavatory, &c.

MARTELL'S & HENNESSY'S BRANDIES.

Charrington's Old, Mild & Pale Ales.

All Liqueurs Kept. Cigars of the Finest Brands.

Uam Var Scotch, Haig and Haig, Claymore, Glen Tuckey, Highland Dirk, Mountain Dew, Lismore's, Walker's, Dewar's, Buchanan's, Cabinet Scotch, H. Thompson's and Dunville's Irish Whiskies and other first-class Spirits.

HOT COFFEE AT 6 A.M.

136. A 1916 advertisement for the *Cock Hotel*. A variety of features are listed, most noticeable being the hot coffee served at 6 a.m., this presumably being for early starting workers or night workers on their way home. Billiard saloons were a popular attraction at this time. It also appeared to be the fashion to advertise a wide variety of whiskies. This may have been a way of reviving the spirits of those engaged in munitions or war work at the end of their shift.

137. The Palace variety theatre, next to East Ham station, was a popular place of entertainment in the first decades of this century. All the famous artistes, such as Florrie Forde, appeared here and there were performances twice nightly. The Palace later showed silent films, as the lure of celluloid entertainment overtook that of live performance.

138. In the years just before and after the First World War a newcomer began to appear in high streets all over the country besides the shops. This was the local cinema. After the war the 'Electric' was a pioneer of silent films opening opposite Benstead's piano emporium.

139. In the late 1920s and '30s cinema design became grander, the art deco style with its Egyptian and Inca motifs being very popular. The Carlton in Green Street is a prime example of such a flamboyant building.

140. Other forms of drama and excitement are not so predictably scheduled, but steal up unawares. 'East Ham on Sea' was the title of one postcard published during the floods. This view at Little Ilford, photographed at the lower end of Church Road and Rectory Road in June 1903, shows the extent of flooding by the Roding over its flood plain.

Progress with the People: Home in East Ham

141. Oak Hall, a fine Georgian family dwelling, once graced the High Street. This flank view was taken from Wakefield Street.

142. The front elevation of Oak Hall, a view taken from the first floor of a building on the opposite side of the High Street. This, like the others shown here, was taken in May 1936 shortly before the house was demolished. The poster on the right-hand side is for the cinema showing of *Charlie Chan's Secret*.

143. A last glimpse of the rear of the house, before it fell prey to the pressures of commercialisation.

144. The great acceleration in house-building which started at the beginning of the 20th century is well illustrated in these 'before and after' scenes from an Edwardian magazine.

145. High Street South, once a lonely road across the East Ham levels, is seen here in 1920. The area is now well-populated with buses and trams serving the transport needs of the people. The Town Hall can be seen in the background.

146. Near the junction with High Street South a tram is approaching. On the left a labour exchange has been opened to help men back from the First World War to find employment.

147. Bartle Avenue, the 'To Let' sign serves as a reminder that for many years the most common form of house transaction was letting – the rent book paying a central part in most people's budgets. A neighbour has drawn back a curtain to see what the photographer is doing, whilst a horse and cart make a delivery in the background.

148. Thorpe Road, a respectable thoroughfare, conventiently placed near the shops, services and transport links of East Ham. Note the well-groomed appearance of the children and the kerbside trees, almost beyond sapling stage.

149. Altmore Avenue was not far from the High Street. The well-dressed children, with their hoops and bicycle, lining up across the road, show that the avenue's inhabitants were comparatively affluent.

150. Ruskin Avenue was north of East Ham station and south-east of Woodgrange Park. The scene shows plenty of activity – an old lady goes about her business as assorted youngsters study the photographer. The girl on the left looks too neatly dressed in white to be playing outside. One of the boys on the right holds a jar on a string and is probably setting out to catch tiddlers in the pond in the park.

151. Two views of Plashet Grove. In effect this was almost a main road because of the tram tracks (single lines in the narrowest part). However, the trees and the curve of the road made it a pleasant place to live.

152. Another part of Plashet Grove.

153. Plashet shopping area.

154. Windsor Road on the Woodgrange Estate. The estate, part of which was in East Ham, was a superior development on the site of the Woodgrange House and grounds. The developer, Cameron Corbett, also built estates in Ilford. Between 1877 and 1892, 1,160 houses were built. The peak year for building activity was 1881, after which recession, lasting until 1890, delayed completion of the estate. Attempts at landscaping included planting garden hedges and lime trees at the front of the properties.

155. A close-up of no. 56 Windsor Road showing the impressive details of the front elevation.

156. Hilda Road, a cul-de-sac with its flourishing saplings, was a very pleasant place to live.

157. The numerous houses that were built, street after street, in Manor Park were less generously planned than those on the Woodgrange Estate, but were nevertheless convenient and economic. First Avenue is a prime example of such development.

158. Like its neighbours, Third Avenue in Manor Park branched off the Romford Road, which had excellent shopping facilities.

159. Iron railings and Venetian blinds would seem to be *de rigeur* in Edwardian Herbert Road.

160. Sherringham Avenue in 1910. At the top ends of the roads in this group in Manor Park were the gates, sheds and yards leading to the premises of businesses in the Romford Road. The title 'Avenue' is not yet justified, since it will be a few years before the flimsy saplings become sturdy trees.

161. This aerial view of Manor Park, taken in 1926, shows how the railway line has affected the grid layout of the streets, leaving a triangular plot for the school buildings.

162. This picture of Manor Park was taken in 1903 and shows the comparative newness of the suburb. It was taken in High Street near the *Ruskin Arms*.

163. The Broadway, Manor Park, is a hive of activity about 1911. Robert Hassell, pawnbroker, at nos. 703-5, offers his services as a moneylender.

164. The multiple stores have moved into Romford Road by the date of this picture. Lilley and Skinner and John Sainsbury ply their trade among the small, independent retailers of Manor Park.

165. Disabled youngsters from the area enjoy an outing to Loughton on the edge of Epping Forest in September 1912.

Civic Pride: The Second World War

The Second World War showed the strength of the English local government system as it existed at the time. Most local authorities were of exactly the right size to motivate their inhabitants to fight for a system that they could see in action. Civic pride played an outstanding part in beating off the Nazi threat in East Ham, helping people to carry on through the worst bombardments, repair the extensive damage to the best of their ability and generally to foster good morale in the neighbourhood. Looking at the record of damage and destruction that follows it is to be wondered that East Ham was able to keep smiling through.

The proximity of East Ham to the Thames, the Docks and many other strategic targets for the German bombers meant that it was in the centre of an area which sufferred severe damage. Many of its citizens were killed during the Blitz on the capital and later rocket bombardments.

A total of 1,454 air raid incidents were recorded. Many more reports were received, however, which dealt with damage at a distance from the incidents and some reports related to more than one missile, especially in the case of incendiary bombs:

High explosive bombs (including unexploded)	742 incidents
Mines (including unexploded)	37 incidents
Incendiary bombs	11,610 incidents
V1 Flying bombs	36 incidents
V2 Long range rockets	20 incidents

The figure under incendiary bombs is not complete since many were dealt with or burnt out, without being reported. The estimated total that fell is 160,000.

Air Raid Casualties

1st phase bombs, incendiaries & mines	391 killed	470 seriously injured	780 slightly injured
2nd phase V1 flying bombs	80 killed	180 seriously injured	507 slightly injured
3rd phase V2 long range rockets	52 killed	118 seriously injured	460 slightly injured
Total	523 killed	768 seriously injured	1,747 slightly injured

166. The City of London cemetery gates and main entrance, photographed in 1943. Hundreds of wartime casualties were buried here.

167. The personnel of East Ham borough official stretcher party no. 23, who carried out their important task quietly and efficiently, sometimes under dangerous circumstances.

WELL CONSTRUCTED

AIR RAID SHELTER

Available to Customers

IN STOCK TO-DAY

100 STIRRUP PUMPS, 29/6

SPLINTEX NET for windows
6¾d. AND 1/- PER YARD

Shelter Mattresses 15/-
Leatherette Bases

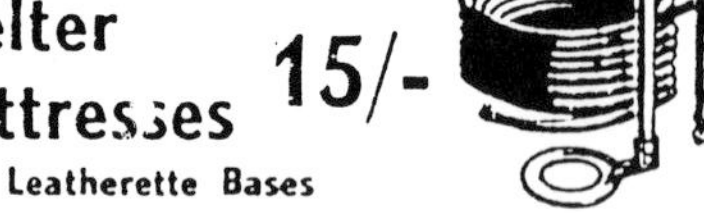

Folding Shelter Chairs, 6/6

Perfection Oil Cookers
on Porcelain Enamel Stands

2-Burner Stove	3-Burner Stove
£5 5s. 0d.	£6 17s. 6d.

BROADWAY Tel. MARyland 5555 STRATFORD

Don't Try Bomb Dodging!

It is simpler to shelter in a Simplex Shelter.

MAXIMUM PROTECTION AND SECURITY.
— MINIMUM RISK AND COST. —
The Lowest Life Insurance Premium for the best present-day Life Policy.

LIMITED STOCK AVAILABLE — IMMEDIATE DELIVERY

Sunken Type—9" Concrete Walls, 6" Heavy reinforced concrete semi-arched Splinter and Bullet-proof Roof.

A WATER-TIGHT GARDEN FORTRESS

Prices to suit everyone's pockets

CREDIT TERMS ARRANGED

SEE IT AT—

SIMPLEX SHELTER CO. DEPOT,
43, CLARENCE AVENUE,
GANT'S HILL CORNER, ILFORD

NO EVENING BUSES AFTER 11 PM

All Central Area buses (those routes numbered **1 to 299**) now cease running at varying times between **10** p.m. and **11** p.m., except on the following routes, on which all night-services will continue to be provided: 11, 17, and 290 to 299 inclusive.

Last buses serving central London leave the out-of-town termini at about 10 p.m. and pass through the central area at about 10.30 p.m.

On many routes the last bus does not make a full journey to the terminus for the route.

A further statement will be issued later announcing the restrictions on evening trolley-buses and trams.

LONDON  TRANSPORT

LW 210/40

168. One of the features of the Second World War was the newspaper advertising which concentrated on wartime necessities. In addition various official notices, warnings and advice from the government kept the public informed about changes affecting everyday life.

169. East Ham civil defence workers present themselves on parade in their decontamination suits.

170. An army weapons column passes through High Street North, bound for the docks and possibly France. The photographer took this unusual photo from above the shops opposite the Premier Cinema.

WILSON AND WHITWORTH, LTD.,

PRINTING IN ALL ITS BRANCHES Neatly and Promptly Executed at Reasonable Prices.

"EXPRESS" OFFICE, 201 AND 203, HIGH STREET NORTH, EAST HAM.

THE BOROUGH OF EAST HAM, WEST HAM

AND

Telephones:
East Ham Office—EAST HAM 529.
Stratford Office—EAST 932.

Stratford Express.

PUBLISHED MONDAY, WEDNESDAY AND FRIDAY.

Telephones:
East Ham Office—EAST HAM 529.
Stratford Office—EAST 932.